Strum It! Guitar

Christmas Songs
For Guitar

T0045097

ISBN 0-634-01870-1

HAL•LEONARD®
CORPORATION

7777 W. BLUEMOUND RD. P.O. BOX 13819 MILWAUKEE, WI 53213

Visit Hal Leonard Online at
www.halleonard.com

Christmas Songs For Guitar

Contents

HOW TO USE THIS BOOK

Strum It!™ is the series designed especially to get you playing (and singing!) along with your favorite songs. The idea is simple—the songs are arranged using their original keys in *lead sheet* format, giving you the chords for each song, beginning to end. The melody and lyrics are also shown to help you keep your spot and sing along.

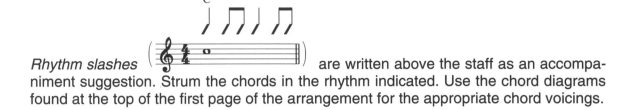

Rhythm slashes are written above the staff as an accompaniment suggestion. Strum the chords in the rhythm indicated. Use the chord diagrams found at the top of the first page of the arrangement for the appropriate chord voicings.

Additional Musical Definitions

⊓	• Downstroke
∨	• Upstroke
D.S. al Coda	• Go back to the sign (𝄋), then play until the measure marked *"To Coda,"* then skip to the section labelled *"Coda."*
D.C. al Fine	• Go back to the beginning of the song and play until the measure marked *"Fine"* (end).
cont. rhy. sim.	• Continue using similar rhythm pattern.
N.C.	• Instrument is silent (drops out).
𝄆 ⁄⁄⁄⁄ 𝄇	• Repeat measures between signs.
1. 2.	• When a repeated section has different endings, play the first ending only the first time and the second ending only the second time.

Almost Day

Words and Music by Huddie Ledbetter

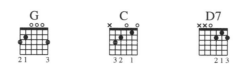

Verse
Moderate Square Dance

1. Chick-ens a-crowin' for mid-night, _ it's al-most day. Chick-ens a-crowin' for
2. *See Additional Lyrics*

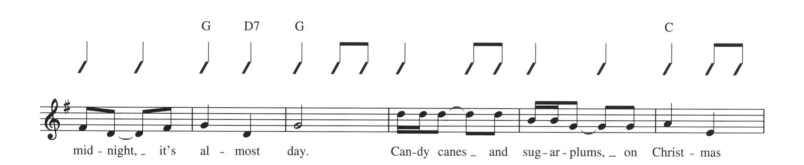

mid-night, _ it's al-most day. Can-dy canes _ and sug-ar-plums, _ on Christ-mas

Day. Can-dy canes _ and sug-ar-plums, _ on Christ-mas Day. Day.

Additional Lyrics

2. Mama'll stuff a turkey on Christmas Day.
Mama'll stuff a turkey on Christmas Day.
Santa Claus is coming on Christmas Day.
Santa Claus is coming on Christmas Day.

Because It's Christmas
(For All the Children)

Music by Barry Manilow
Lyric by Bruce Sussman and Jack Feldman

Verse
Moderately Slow

1. To-night the stars __ shine __ for the chil - dren and light the way for dreams to
2. *See Additional Lyrics*

fly. To-night our love comes wrapped in _____ rib - bons.

The world is right and hopes are high. And from a dark __ and frost - ed

win - dow a child __ ap - pears to search __ the sky be - cause __ it's

1. Christ-mas, be - cause it's Christ-mas. **2.** Christ-mas for now __ and for-ev - er for all __ of the

Additional Lyrics

2. Tonight belongs to all the children.
   Tonight their joy rings through the air.
   And so, we send our tender blessings
   To all the children ev'rywhere
   To see the smiles and hear the laughter,
   A time to give, a time to share
   Because it's Christmas for now and forever
   For all of the children in us all.

C-H-R-I-S-T-M-A-S

Words by Jenny Lou Carson
Music by Eddy Arnold

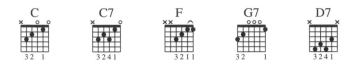

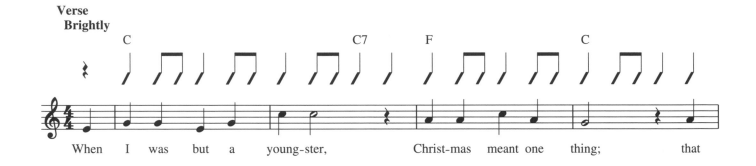

Verse
Brightly

When I was but a young-ster, Christ-mas meant one thing; that

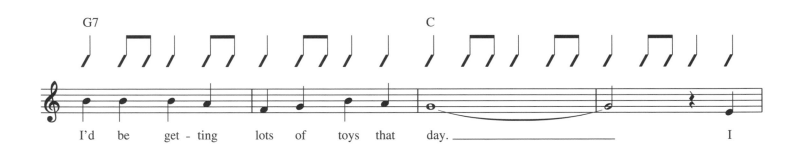

I'd be get - ting lots of toys that day. _____ I

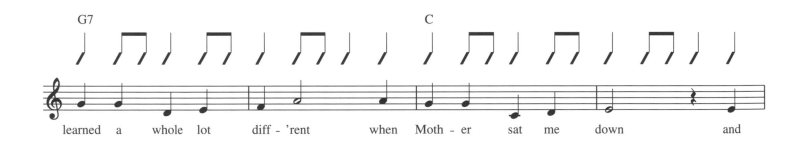

learned a whole lot diff - 'rent when Moth - er sat me down and

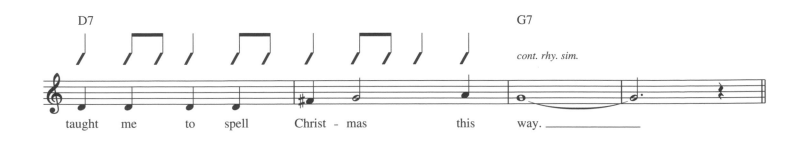

taught me to spell Christ - mas this way. _____

Chorus

The Christmas Song
(Chestnuts Roasting On an Open Fire)

Music and Lyric by Mel Torme and Robert Wells

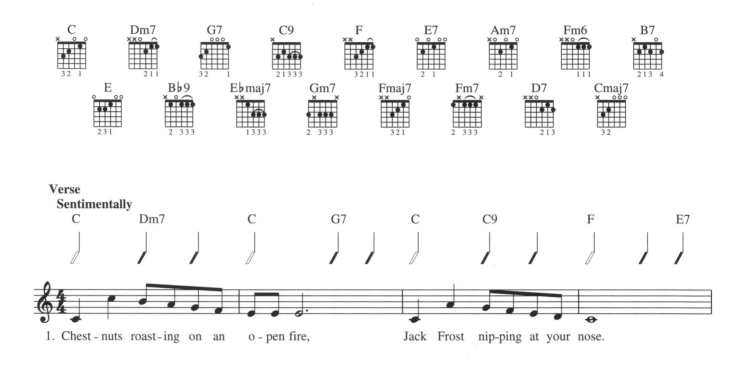

Verse
Sentimentally

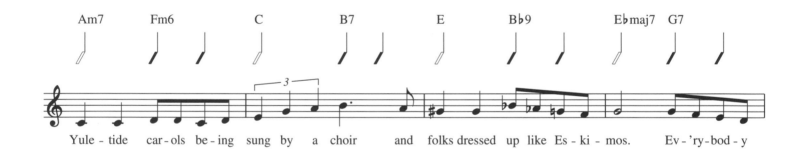

1. Chest - nuts roast - ing on an o - pen fire, Jack Frost nip-ping at your nose.

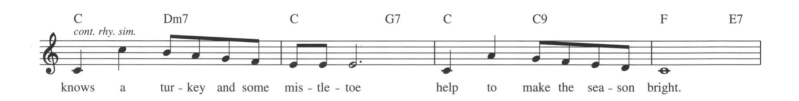

Yule - tide car - ols be - ing sung by a choir and folks dressed up like Es - ki - mos. Ev - 'ry-bod - y

knows a tur - key and some mis - tle - toe help to make the sea - son bright.

Ti - ny tots with their eyes all a - glow will find it hard to sleep to -

Bridge

night. They know that San - ta's on his way. He's load - ed

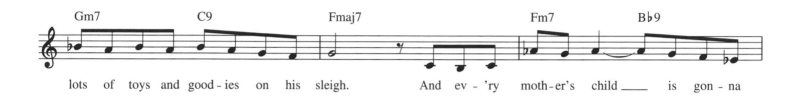

lots of toys and good-ies on his sleigh. And ev-'ry moth-er's child ___ is gon - na

spy ___ to see if rein - deer ___ real - ly know how to fly. 2. And

Verse

so I'm of - fer - ing this sim - ple phrase to kids from one to nine - ty - two. Al -

though it's been said man - y times, man - y ways, "Mer - ry Christ - mas to you."

Do They Know It's Christmas?

Words and Music by M. Ure and B. Geldof

get this year ___ is life. ___   Oh. _____ Where

noth - ing ev - er grows, ___   no rain or riv - ers flow, _

___ do they know it's Christ - mas - time at ___ all? _____

Here's to you, raise a glass for ev - 'ry - one; here's to them un - der -

neath that burn - ing sun. Do they know it's Christ - mas - time at ___

all? _____

Outro

Feed the world. _____

Feed the world, _____ let them know it's Christ - mas - time a -

Repeat & Fade

gain.   Let them know it's Christ - mas - time a -

Feliz Navidad

Music and Lyrics by Jose Feliciano

Frosty the Snow Man

Words and Music by Steve Nelson and Jack Rollins

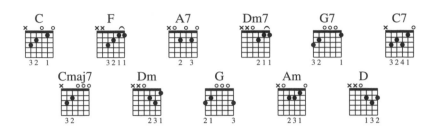

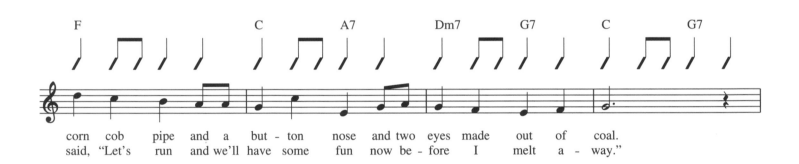

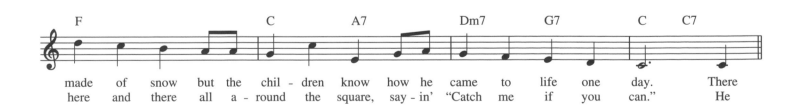

Bridge

must have been some mag - ic in that old silk hat they found, for
let them down the streets of town right to the traf - fic cop, and he

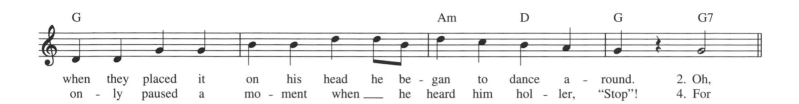

when they placed it on his head he be - gan to dance a - round. 2. Oh,
on - ly paused a mo - ment when ___ he heard him hol - ler, "Stop"! 4. For

Verse

Frost - y the snow - man was a - live as he could be, and the
Frost - y the snow - man had to hur - ry on his way, but he

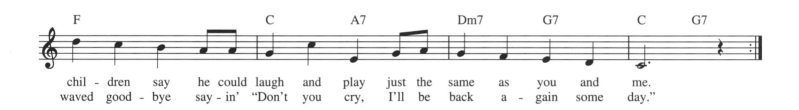

chil - dren say he could laugh and play just the same as you and me.
waved good - bye say - in' "Don't you cry, I'll be back a - gain some day."

Outro

Thump-et - y thump thump, thump-et - y thump thump, look at Frost - y go.

Thump-et - y thump thump, thump-et - y thump thump, o - ver the hills of snow.

Grandma Got Run Over By a Reindeer

Words and Music by Randy Brooks

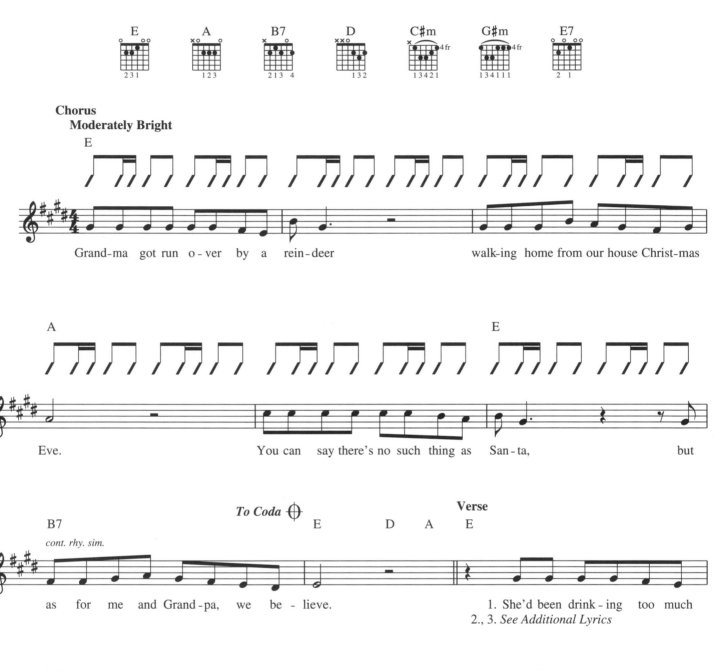

snow. When we found her Christ-mas morn-ing

at the scene of the at - tack, she had hoof-prints on her

1., 2. **3.** **D.C. al Coda**

fore-head, and in - crim - i - nat-ing Claus marks on her back. elves.

Coda

Outro-Chorus

lieve. Grand-ma got run o - ver by a rein-deer

walk-ing home from our house Christ-mas Eve. You can say there's no such thing as

San-ta, but as for me and Grand-pa, we be - lieve. _____

Additional Lyrics

2. Now we're all so proud of Grandpa.
   He's been taking it so well.
   See him in there watching football,
   Drinking beer and playing cards with Cousin Mel.
   It's not Christmas without Grandma.
   All the family's dressed in black,
   And we just can't help but wonder:
   Should we open up her gifts or send them back?

3. Now the goose is on the table,
   And the pudding made of fig.
   And the blue and silver candles,
   That would just have matched the hair in Grandma's wig.
   I've warned all my friends and neighbors.
   Better watch out for yourselves.
   They should never give a license
   To a man who drives a sleigh and plays with elves.

Grandma's Killer Fruitcake

Words and Music by Elmo Shropshire and Rita Abrams

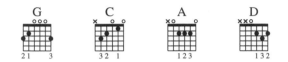

Intro
Country Polka

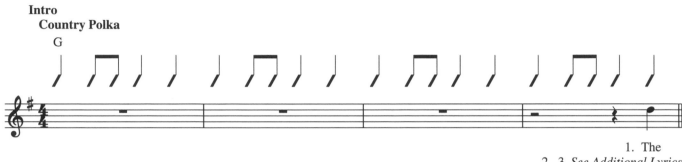

1. The
2., 3. *See Additional Lyrics*

Verse

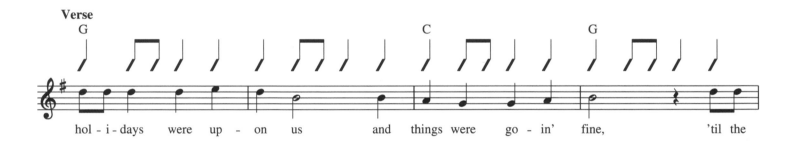

hol - i - days were up - on us and things were go - in' fine, 'til the

day I heard the door - bell and a chill ran up my spine. I

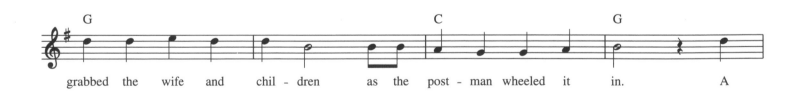

grabbed the wife and chil - dren as the post - man wheeled it in. A

year - ly Christ - mas night - mare has just come back a - gain. It was

Chorus

hard - er than the head of Un - cle Buck - y, heav - y as a Ser - mon of

Preach - er Luck - y. One's e - nough to give the whole state of Ken - tuck - y a

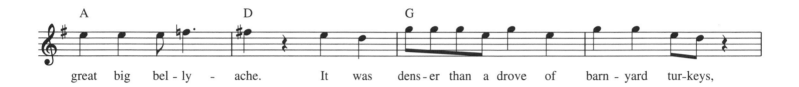

great big bel - ly - ache. It was dens - er than a drove of barn - yard tur-keys,

tough - er than a truck load of all beef jerk - y. Dri - er than a drought in

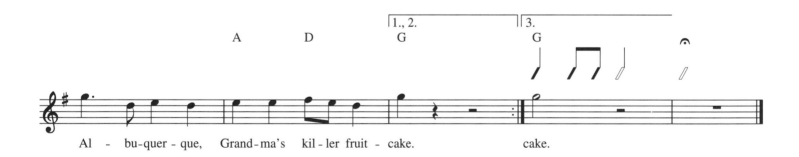

Al - bu-quer - que, Grand-ma's kil - ler fruit - cake. cake.

Additional Lyrics

2. Now I've had to swallow some marginal fare at our family feast.
   I even downed Aunt Dolly's possom pie just to keep the family peace.
   I winced at Wilma's gizzard mousse, but said it tasted fine,
   But that lethal weapon that Grandma bakes is where I draw the line.

3. It's early Christmas morning, the phone rings us awake.
   It's Grandma, Pa, she wants to know how'd we like the cake.
   "Well, Grandma, I never. Uh, we couldn't. It was, uh, unbelievable, that's for shore.
   What's that you say? Oh, no Grandma, Puh-leez don't send us more!"

The Greatest Gift of All

Words and Music by John Jarvis

Through the win - dow   I ___ can   see ___   snow be - gin   to   fall.

Know - ing you're in ___ love with   me ___ is the great - est   gift   of ___ all.

Verse

3. Just be - fore   I   go   to   sleep ___   I   hear a church bell   ring.

Mer - ry Christ - mas   ev - 'ry - one ___   is   the song   it ___ sings.

So   I   say   a   si - lent   prayer ___   for   crea - tures great   and   small.

Peace on earth   good _   will   to   men   is   the great - est   gift   of ___ all.   Peace on earth   good _

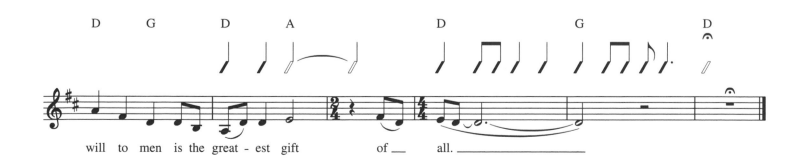

will   to   men   is   the great - est   gift   of ___ all. ___

Happy Hanukkah, My Friend
(The Hanukkah Song)

Words and Music by Douglas Alan Konecky and Justin Wilde

Verse
Moderately

1. Spin the drei-del, light the lights, ev-'ry-one stay home to-night. The
2. *See Additional Lyrics*

sto-ry is told, __ the young and the old __ to-geth - er. As

twi-light greets the set-ting sun, light the can-dles one by one. Re -

mem-ber the past, __ tra-di-tions that last __ for-ev - er.

Chorus

Come, let's share the joy of Ha-nuk - kah. May our friend-ship grow, __

as the can-dles glow. _____ Oh, won't you come and share the joy of

Ha - nuk - kah, { and we'll cel - e - brate _ as on - ly friends _ can do. ____
{ and we're hop - ing all ___ you're wish - ing for ___ comes true. ___

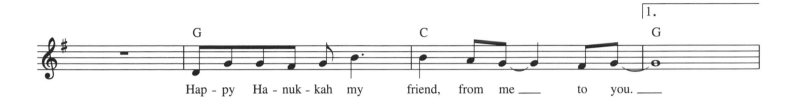

Hap - py Ha - nuk - kah my friend, from me ____ to you. ____

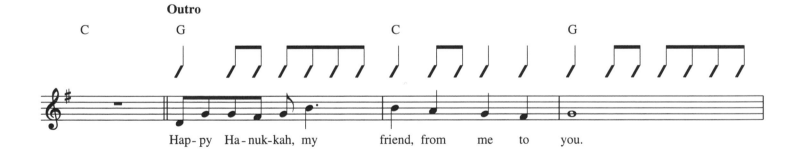

Hap- py Ha-nuk-kah, my friend, from me to you.

Additional Lyrics

2. Candlelight or star above,
   Messages of peace and love;
   Their meaning is clear, we all were put here as brothers.
   So let's begin with you and me,
   Let friendship shine eternally,
   May this holiday enlighten the way for others.

Happy Holiday

from the Motion Picture Irving Berlin's HOLIDAY INN

Words and Music by Irving Berlin

He

Words by Richard Mullen
Music by Jack Richards

A Holly Jolly Christmas

Music and Lyrics by Johnny Marks

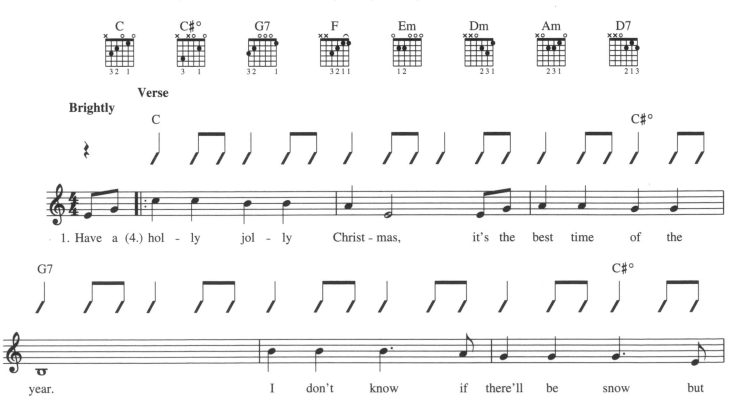

Happy Xmas
(War Is Over)

Words and Music by John Lennon and Yoko Ono

Verse

G .... **Am**

Christ-mas .... for weak and for strong, ... the rich and the
(War is o - ver if you want it;

D7 .... **Am** .... **D7** .... **G**

poor ones, ... the road is so ___ long. .... And so, hap-py
war is o - ver now.

C .... **Dm**

Christ-mas .... for black and for white, ... for the yel-low and
War is o - ver if you want it;

G7 .... **C**

red ones, ... let's stop all the fights. _____ A mer-ry, mer-ry
war is o - ver now. _____)

Chorus

F .... **G**

Christ-mas .... and a hap-py new year, ... let's hope it's a

D.S. al Coda

Dm .... **F** .... **C** **D7**

good one _____ with-out an - y fear. .... 3. And so this is

Coda

C .... **D7** .... **G**

fear. .... (War is o - ver

Am .... **D7** .... **Am D7 G D7 Am G**

if you want it; war is o - ver now. _____)

(There's No Place Like)
Home for the Holidays

Words by Al Stillman
Music by Robert Allen

home-made pump-kin pie. From Penn-syl-van-ia folks are trav-'lin' down to
wel-come with your heart. From Cal-i-for-nia to New Eng-land down to

Dix-ie's sun-ny shore;}
Dix-ie's sun-ny shore;} from At-lan-tic to Pa-ci-fic, gee, the

Chorus

traf-fic is ter-ri-fic. Oh, there's no place like home for the

hol-i-days, _____ 'cause no mat-ter how far a-way you roam, _____ if you

want to be hap-py in a mil-lion ways, _____ for the

hol-i-days you can't beat home, sweet home. _____ Oh, there's

can't beat home, sweet home. _____

Hymne

By Vangelis

I Heard the Bells on Christmas Day

Words by Henry Wadsworth Longfellow
Adapted by Johnny Marks
Music by Johnny Marks

Additional Lyrics

2. I thought as now this day had come,
   The belfries of all Christendom
   Had rung so long the unbroken song
   Of peace on earth, good will to men.

3. And in despair I bowed my head;
   "There is no peace on earth," I said,
   "For hate is strong, and mocks the song
   Of peace on earth, good will to men."

4. Then pealed the bells more loud and deep;
   "God is not dead, nor noth He sleep.
   The wrong shall fail, the right prevail
   With peace on earth, good will to men."

I Saw Mommy Kissing Santa Claus

Words and Music by Tommie Connor

I'll Be Home for Christmas

Words and Music by Kim Gannon and Walter Kent

I'm Spending Christmas With You

Words and Music by Tom Occhipinti

Verse
Moderately Slow

1. The snow is gent - ly fall-ing, the night is so cold. ___ The moon shines ___ on the
2. *See Additional Lyrics*

snow cov - ered trees. The road seemed like _____ for - ev - er, ___ but I'm

cont. rhy. sim.

fi - nal - ly home. ___ We're a - lone on this Christ - mas Eve.

Chorus

I'm spend - ing Christ - mas _____ with ___ you. _____ 'Tis the

sea - son ___ when love is re - newed. _____ My hol - i - day

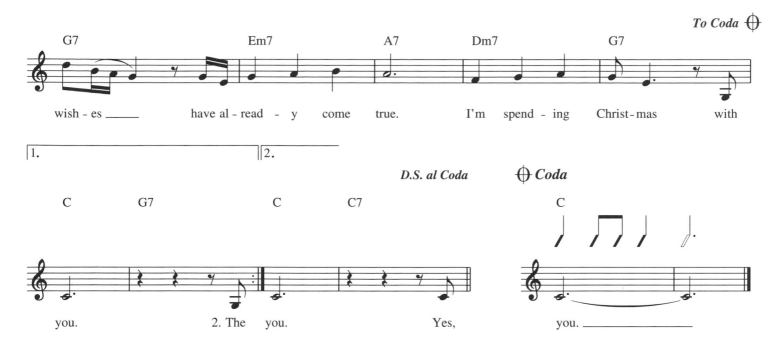

Additional Lyrics

2. The fireplace is burning and your hands feel so warm.
   We're hanging popcorn on the tree.
   I take you in my arms, your lips touch mine.
   It feels like our first Christmas Eve.

Jingle-Bell Rock

Words and Music by Joe Beal and Jim Boothe

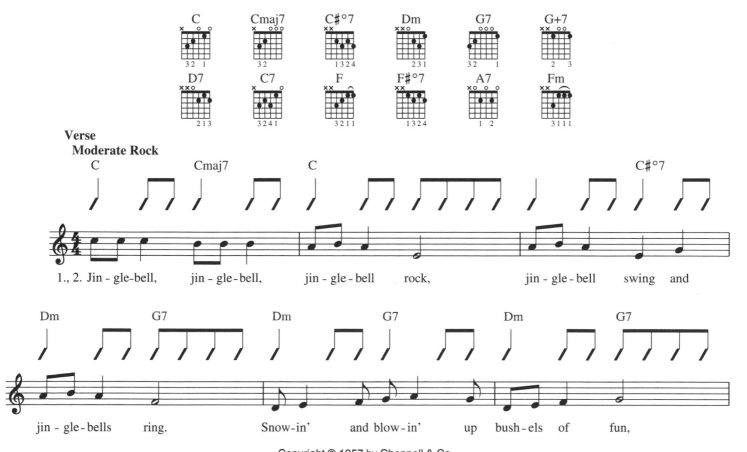

now the jin-gle-hop has be - gun. Jin - gle-bell, jin-gle-bell,

jin-gle-bell rock, jin-gle-bells chime in jin-gle-bell time. Dan-cin' and pran-cin' in

Jin - gle-bell Square in the fros - ty air. What a bright time, it's the

right time to rock the night a - way. Jin - gle - bell time is a

swell time to go gli-din' in a one horse sleigh.

Outro

Gid-dy-ap, jin-gle horse pick up your feet, jin-gle a - round the clock.

Mix and min-gle in a jin-gle-in' beat, that's the { jin - gle-bell rock. / jin-gle-bell,

that's the jin-gle-bell, that's the jin-gle-bell rock.

It's Beginning to Look Like Christmas

By Meredith Willson

Let It Snow! Let It Snow! Let It Snow!

Words by Sammy Cahn
Music by Jule Styne

A Marshmallow World

Words by Carl Sigman
Music by Peter De Rose

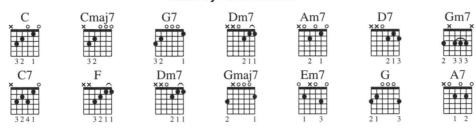

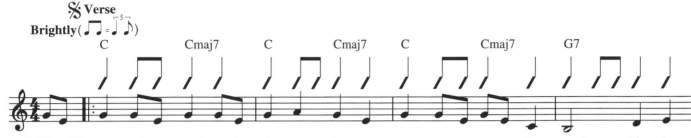

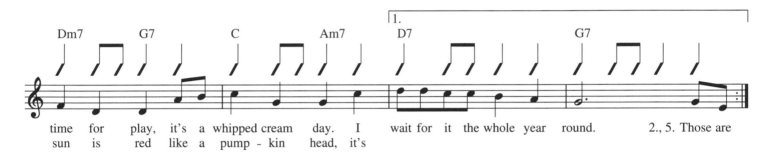

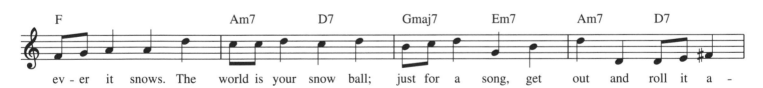

The Most Wonderful Time of the Year

Words and Music by Eddie Pola and George Wyle

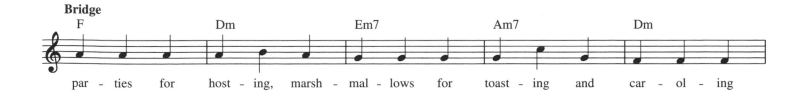

Bridge

par - ties for host - ing, marsh - mal - lows for toast - ing and car - ol - ing

out in the snow. There'll be scar - y ghost stor - ies and

D.S. al Coda

tales of the glo - ries of Christ - mas - es long, long a - go. _____ 3. It's the

Coda
Outro

most won - der - ful time, it's the most won - der - ful

time. It's the most won - der - ful time _____

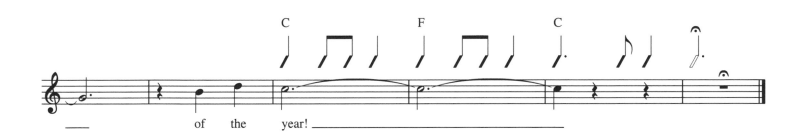

_____ of the year! _____

Additional Lyrics

2. It's the hap-happiest season of all,
   With those holiday greetings
   And gay happy meetings
   When friends come to call.
   It's the hap-happiest season of all.

3. It's the most wonderful time of the year.
   There'll be much mistletoeing
   And hearts will be glowing
   When loved ones are near.
   It's the most wonderful time of the year.

My Favorite Things

from THE SOUND OF MUSIC

Lyrics by Oscar Hammerstein II
Music by Richard Rodgers

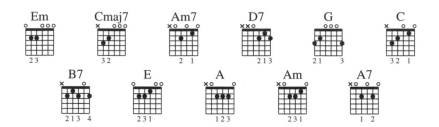

Verse
Lively, With Spirit

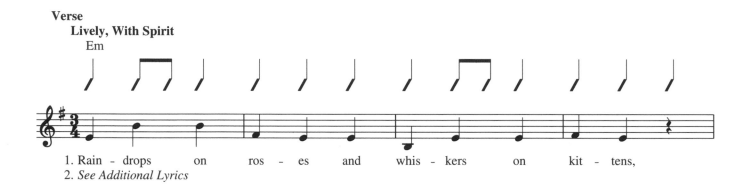

1. Rain - drops on ros - es and whis - kers on kit - tens,
2. *See Additional Lyrics*

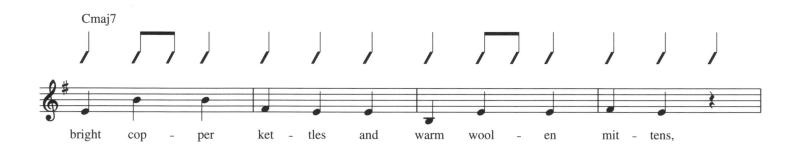

bright cop - per ket - tles and warm wool - en mit - tens,

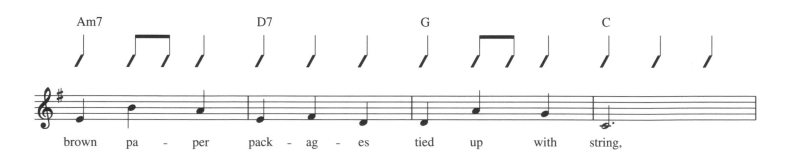

brown pa - per pack - ag - es tied up with string,

these are a few of my fa - vor - ite things.

Verse

3. Girls in white dress-es with blue sat-in sash-es, snow-flakes that

stay on my nose and eye-lash-es, sil-ver white win-ters that

melt in-to springs, these are a few of my fa-vor-ite

Outro

things. When the dog bites, when the bee stings,

when I'm feel-ing sad, _____ I sim-ply re-

mem-ber my fa-vor-ite things and then I don't feel

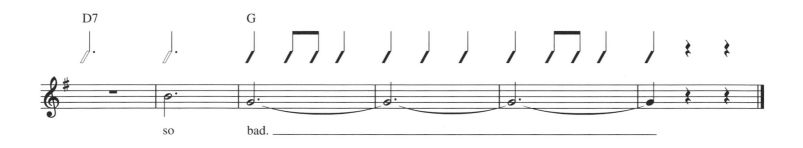

so bad. _____

Additional Lyrics

2. Cream colored ponies and crisp apple strudles,
   Doorbells and sleigh bells and schnitzel with noodles,
   Wild geese that fly with the moon on their wings,
   These are a few of my favorite things.

The Night Before Christmas Song

Music by Johnny Marks
Lyrics adapted by Johnny Marks from Clement Moore's Poem

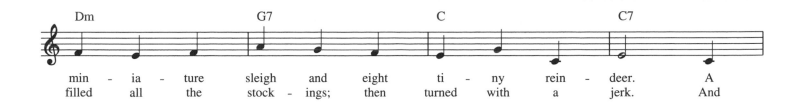

min - ia - ture sleigh and eight ti - ny rein - deer. A
filled all the stock - ings; then turned with a jerk. And

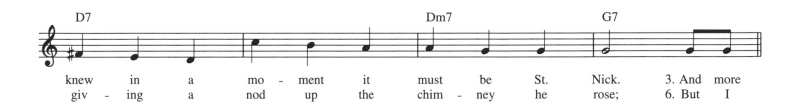

lit - tle old dri - ver so live - ly and quick, I
lay - ing his fin - ger a - side of his nose, then

knew in a mo - ment it must be St. Nick. 3. And more
giv - ing a nod up the chim - ney he rose; 6. But I

Verse

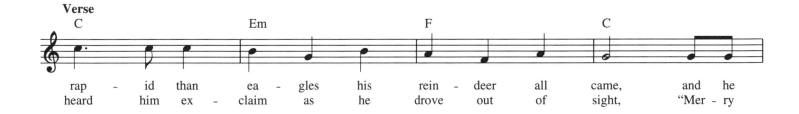

rap - id than ea - gles his rein - deer all came, and he
heard him ex - claim as he drove out of sight, "Mer - ry

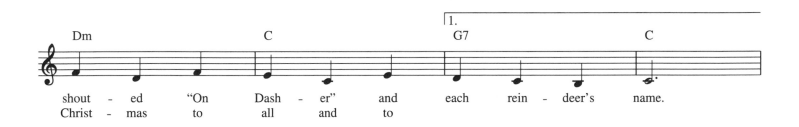

shout - ed "On Dash - er" and each rein - deer's name.
Christ - mas to all and to

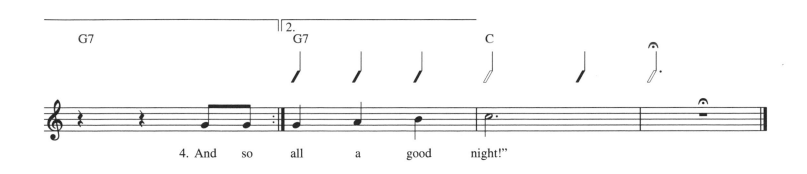

4. And so all a good night!"

Nuttin' for Christmas

Words and Music by Roy Bennett and Sid Tepper

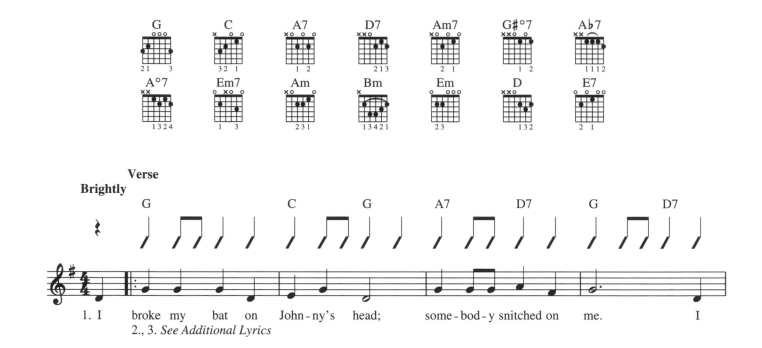

Verse
Brightly

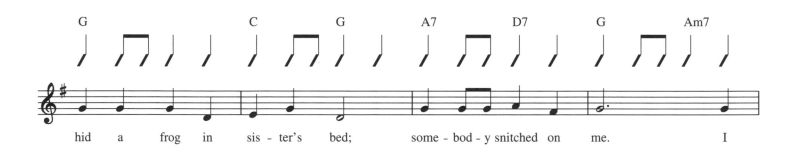

1. I broke my bat on John-ny's head; some-bod-y snitched on me. I
2., 3. *See Additional Lyrics*

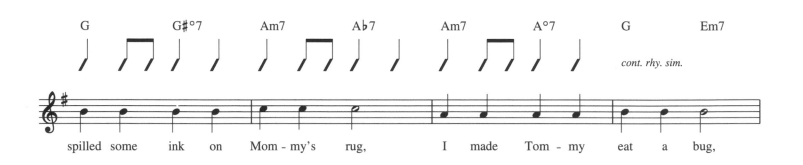

hid a frog in sis-ter's bed; some-bod-y snitched on me. I

spilled some ink on Mom-my's rug, I made Tom-my eat a bug,

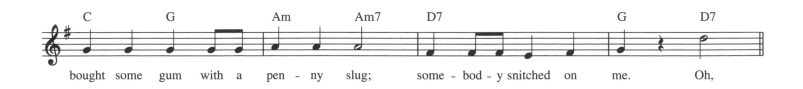

bought some gum with a pen-ny slug; some-bod-y snitched on me. Oh,

Chorus

I'm get-tin' nut-tin' for Christ-mas. Mom - my and

Dad - dy are mad. I'm get-tin' nut-tin' for Christ-mas,

'cause I ain't been nut-tin' but bad. _____ 2. I

Outro

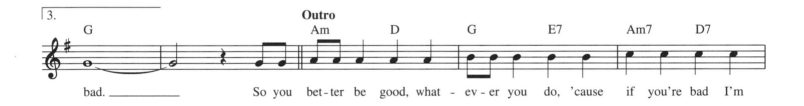

bad. _____ So you bet-ter be good, what - ev - er you do, 'cause if you're bad I'm

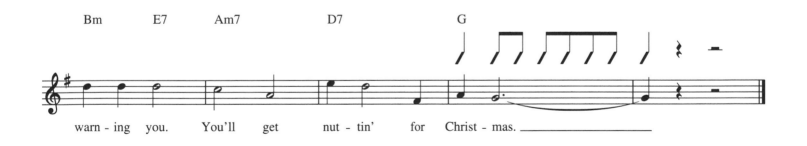

warn-ing you. You'll get nut-tin' for Christ-mas. _____

Additional Lyrics

2. I put a tack on teacher's chair;
Somebody snitched on me.
I tied a knot in Susie's hair;
Somebody snitched on me.
I did a dance on Mommy's plants,
Climbed a tree and tore my pants.
Filled the sugar bowl with ants;
Somebody snitched on me.

3. I won't be seeing Santa Claus;
Somebody snitched on me.
He won't come visit me because
Somebody snitched on me.
Next year, I'll be going straight.
Next year, I'll be good, just wait.
I'd start now but it's too late;
Somebody snitched on me.

Old Toy Trains

Words and Music by Roger Miller

Chorus
Moderately

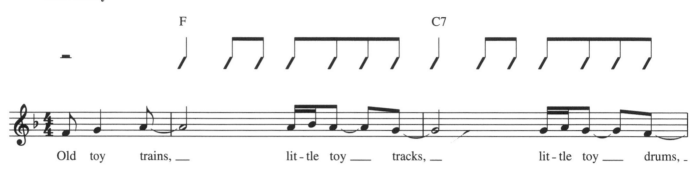

Old toy trains, ___ lit-tle toy ___ tracks, ___ lit-tle toy ___ drums, _

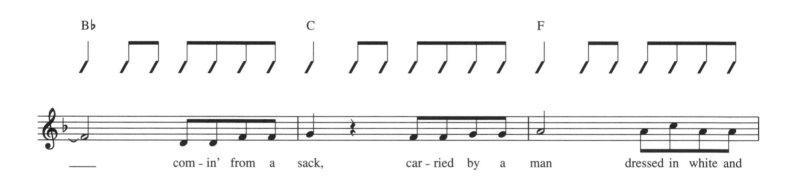

___ com-in' from a sack, car-ried by a man dressed in white and

red. Lit-tle boy ___ don't ___ you think it's time you were in bed? Close your

Bridge

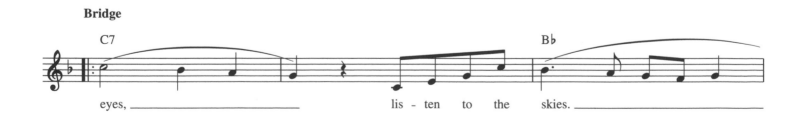

eyes, _____ lis-ten to the skies. _____

All is calm, all is well; soon you'll hear Kris

Chorus

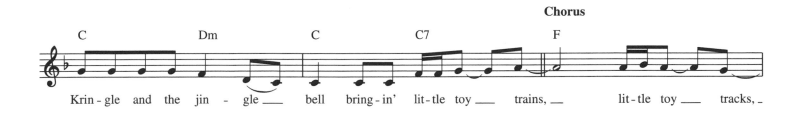

Krin-gle and the jin - gle ___ bell bring-in' lit-tle toy ___ trains, ___ lit-tle toy ___ tracks, ___

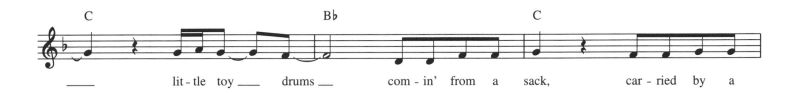

___ lit-tle toy ___ drums ___ com-in' from a sack, car-ried by a

man dressed in white and red. Lit-tle boy ___ don't ___ you think it's time you were in

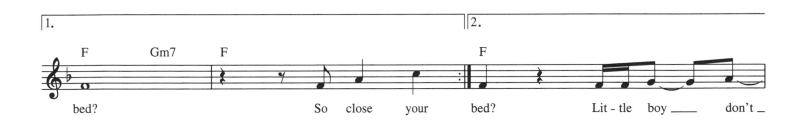

1.
bed?   So close your bed?   Lit-tle boy ___ don't ___

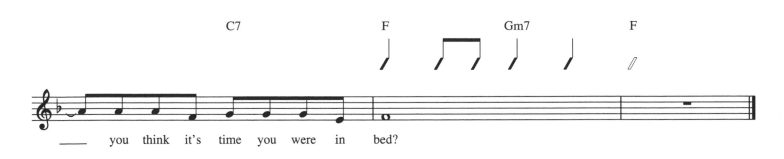

___ you think it's time you were in bed?

Parade of the Wooden Soldiers

English Lyrics by Ballard MacDonald
Music by Leon Jessel

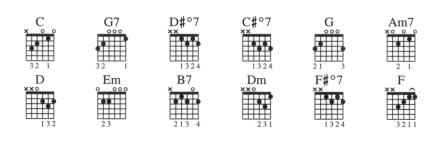

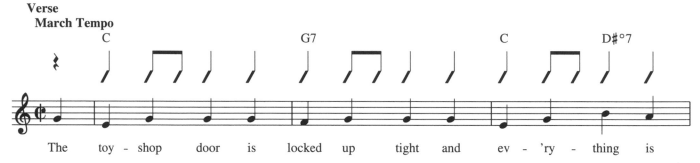

The toy-shop door is locked up tight and ev-'ry-thing is

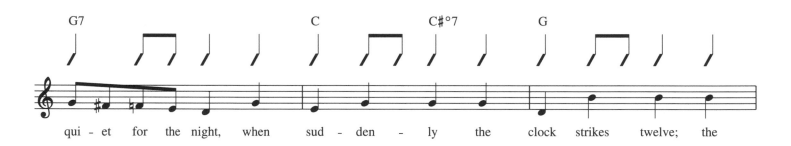

qui-et for the night, when sud-den-ly the clock strikes twelve; the

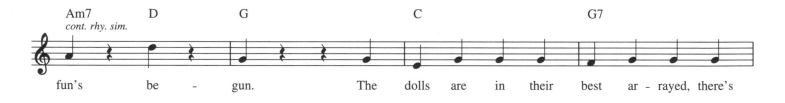

fun's be-gun. The dolls are in their best ar-rayed, there's

going to be a won-der-ful pa-rade. Hark to the drum, oh,

here they come, cries ev-'ry-one!

Chorus

Hear them all cheer - ing, now they are near - ing, there's the cap - tain stiff as starch.

Bay - o - nets flash - ing, mu - sic is crash - ing as the wood - en sol - diers march.

Sa - bres a - click - ing, sol - diers a - wink - ing at each pret - ty lit - tle maid.

Here they come! Here they come! Here they come! Here they come! Wood - en sol - diers on pa - rade.

Day-light is creep - ing, dol - lies are sleep - ing in the toy - shop win - dow fast.

Sol - diers so jol - ly, think of each dol - ly dream - ing of the night that's past.

When in the morn - ing, with-out a warn - ing, toy - man pulls the win - dow shade,

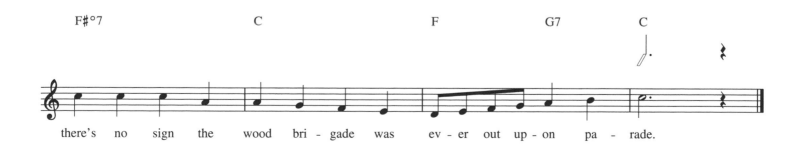

there's no sign the wood bri - gade was ev - er out up - on pa - rade.

55

Pretty Paper

Words and Music by Willie Nelson

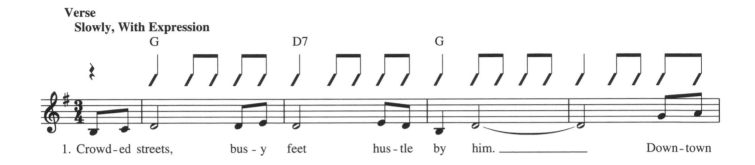

Verse
Slowly, With Expression

1. Crowd-ed streets,   bus-y feet   hus-tle by him. _____   Down-town

shop-pers,   Christ-mas is   nigh. _____   There he

sits   all a-lone   on the side-walk. _____   Hop-ing that

you won't pass him   by. _____   2. Should you   stop;   bet-ter

not,   much too bus-y. _____   You're in a hur-ry, my

how time does fly.____ In the dis - tance the

ring - ing of __ laugh - ter ____ and in the midst of the

Chorus

laugh - ter he cries. ____ Pret - ty pa - per, pret - ty

rib - bons of blue. ____ Wrap your pres - ents to your

dar - ling from you. ____ Pret - ty pen - cils to

write, "I love you." ____ Pret - ty pa - per, pret - ty

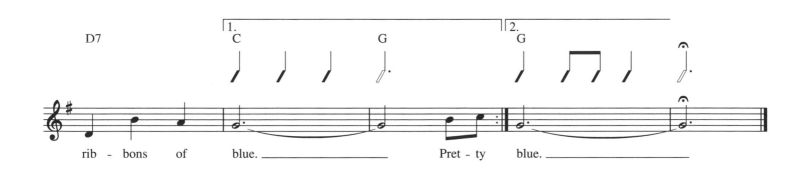

rib - bons of blue. ____ Pret - ty blue. ____

Rockin' Around the Christmas Tree

Music and Lyrics by Johnny Marks

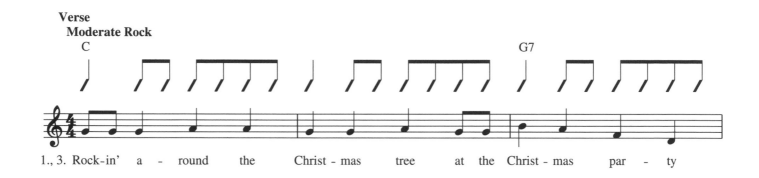

Verse
Moderate Rock

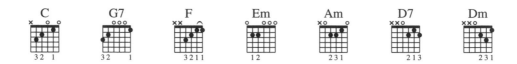

1., 3. Rock-in' a - round the Christ - mas tree at the Christ - mas par - ty

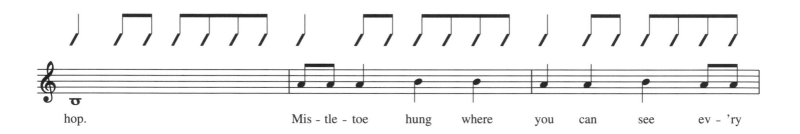

hop. Mis - tle - toe hung where you can see ev - 'ry

cou - ple tries to stop. Rock-in' a - round the

Christ - mas tree, let the Christ - mas spir - it ring. La - ter we'll have some

pump - kin pie and we'll do some car - ol - ing. You will get a

sen - ti - men - tal feel - ing when you hear voic - es sing - ing,

"Let's be jol - ly. Deck the halls with boughs of hol - ly."

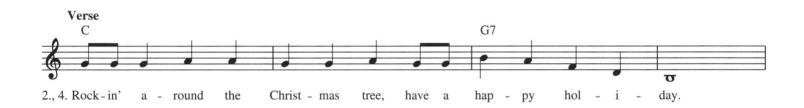

2., 4. Rock - in' a - round the Christ - mas tree, have a hap - py hol - i - day.

Ev - 'ry - one danc - ing mer - ri - ly in the new old fash - ioned way.

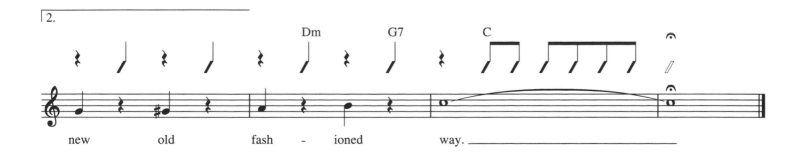

new old fash - ioned way.

Rudolph the Red-Nosed Reindeer

Music and Lyrics by Johnny Marks

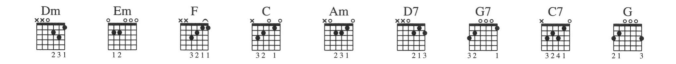

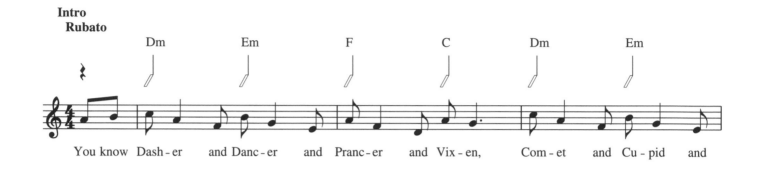

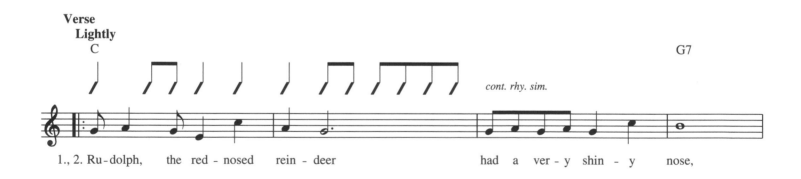

All of the oth - er rein - deer used to laugh and call him names,

they nev - er let poor Ru - dolph join in an - y rein - deer games.

Bridge

Then one fog - gy Christ - mas Eve, San - ta came to say,

"Ru - dolph, with your nose so bright, won't you guide my sleigh to - night?" _

Outro

Then how the rein - deer loved him as they shout - ed out with glee;

1.

"Ru - dolph, the red - nosed rein - deer, you'll go down in his - to - ry!"

2.

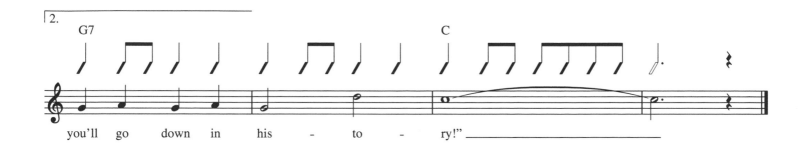

you'll go down in his - to - ry!" _____

Santa Baby

By Joan Javits, Phil Springer and Tony Springer

San - ta ba - by, so hur - ry down the chim - ney to - night. _____

Bridge

Think of all the fun I've missed. _ Think of all the fel - las that I
See Additional Lyrics

have - n't kissed. _ Next year I could be just as good _ if you check off my

Verse

Christ - mas list. 3. San - ta ba - by, I want a yacht and real - ly that's not ____ a lot; ___
6. *See Additional Lyrics*

been an an - gel all year. ___ San - ta ba - by, so hur - ry down the chim - ney to - night. _

1.

2.

Additional Lyrics

4. Santa baby, one little thing I really do need;
   The deed to a platinum mine.
   Santa honey, so hurry down the chimney tonight.

5. Santa cutie and fill my stocking with a duplex and cheques.
   Sign your X on the line.
   Santa cutie, and hurry down the chimney tonight.

Bridge Come and trim my Christmas tree
          With some decorations at Tiffany.
          I really do believe in you.
          Let's see if you believe in me.

6. Santa baby, forgot to mention one little thing, a ring!
   I don't mean on the phone.
   Santa baby, so hurry down the chimney tonight.

Shake Me I Rattle
(Squeeze Me I Cry)

Words and Music by Hal Hackady and Charles Naylor

I could hear her sigh. Shake me I rat - tle, squeeze me I cry. Please take me home and love _ me. 2. I re -

Additional Lyrics

2. I recalled another toy shop on a square so long ago
   Where I saw a little dolly that I wanted so
   I remembered, I remembered how I longed to make it mine.
   And around that other dolly hung another little sign:

3. It was late and snow was falling as the shoppers hurried by,
   Past the girlie at the window with her little head held high.
   They were closing up the toy shop as I hurried through the door.
   Just in time to buy the dolly that her heart was longing for.

Snowfall

Lyrics by Ruth Thornhill
Music by Claude Thornhill

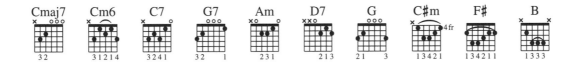

Intro
Moderately

1., 4. Snow - fall, _____ soft - ly, _____

gent - ly _____ drift down. _____

Verse

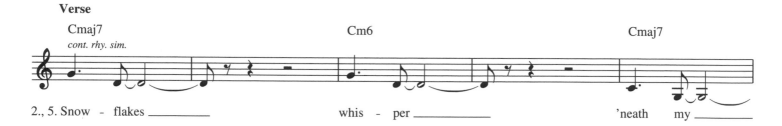

2., 5. Snow - flakes _____ whis - per _____ 'neath my _____

Bridge

win - dow. _____ Cov - 'ring trees

mist - y white. Vel - vet breeze 'round my

Verse

door - step. 3., 6. Gent - ly, _____ soft - ly, _____

1.

si - lent _____ snow - fall! _____

2.

_____

Silver Bells
from the Paramount Picture THE LEMON DROP KID

Words and Music by Jay Livingston and Ray Evans

Additional Lyrics

2. Strings of street lights even stop lights
   Blink a bright red and green,
   As the shoppers rush home with their treasures.
   Hear the snow crunch, see the kids bunch,
   This is Santa's big scene,
   And above all the bustle you hear:

Suzy Snowflake

Words and Music by Sid Tepper and Roy Bennett

That Christmas Feeling

Words and Music by Bennie Benjamin and George Weiss

We Need a Little Christmas

from MAME

Music and Lyric by Jerry Herman

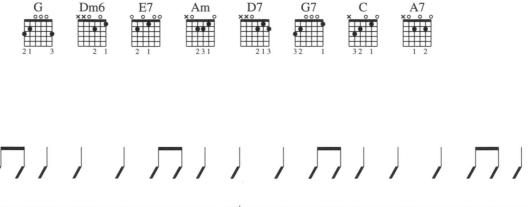

Verse
Brightly

1. Haul out the hol - ly. _____ Put up the
2. *See Additional Lyrics*

tree be - fore my spir - it falls _____ a - gain.

Fill up the stock - ing. _____ I may be

rush - ing things, but deck the halls _____ a - gain

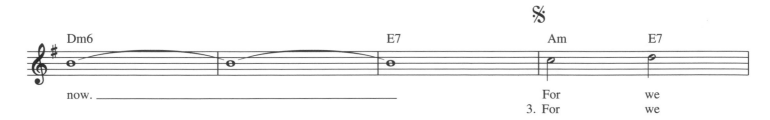

now. _____ For we
3. For we

need a lit - tle Christ - mas, right this ver - y min - ute,
need a lit - tle mu - sic, need a lit - tle laugh - ter,

can - dles in the win - dow, car - ols at the spin - et. Yes, we
need a lit - tle sing - ing, ring - ing through the raft - er. And we

1.

To Coda ⊕

need a lit - tle Christ - mas, right this ver - y min - ute. It
need a lit - tle snap - py "hap - py ev - er

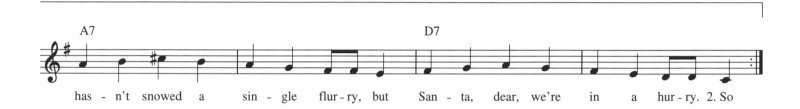

has - n't snowed a sin - gle flur - ry, but San - ta, dear, we're in a hur - ry. 2. So

2.

D.S. al Coda

shoul - der, need a lit - tle Christ - mas now!

⊕ *Coda*

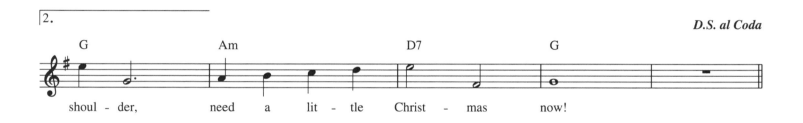

af - ter," need a lit - tle Christ - mas now! _____

Additional Lyrics

2. So climb down the chimney,
Turn on the brightest string of lights I've ever seen.
Slice up the fruitcake.
It's time we hung some tinsel on the evergreen bough.
For I've grown a little leaner, grown a little colder,
Grown a little sadder, grown a little older,
And I need a little angel, sitting on my shoulder,
Need a little Christmas now!

What Are You Doing New Year's Eve?

By Frank Loesser

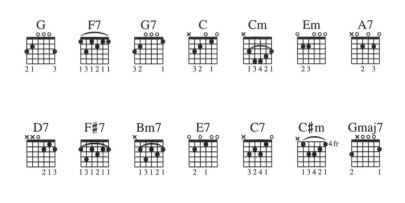

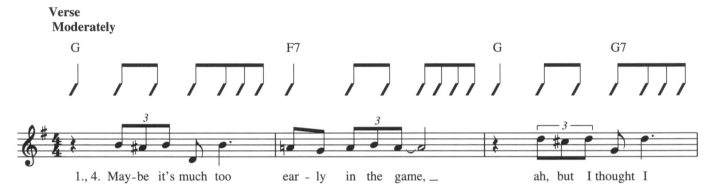

1., 4. May-be it's much too early in the game, _ ah, but I thought I

ask you just the same, _ what are you do-ing new year's, New Year's

Eve? 2., 5. Won-der whose arms will hold you good and tight, _

when it's ex-act-ly twelve o'-clock that night, _ wel-com-ing in the

Bridge

new year, New Year's Eve. May-be I'm cra-zy

to sup - pose I'd ev - er be the one you chose

out of the thou - sand in - vi - ta - tions you'll re -

Verse

ceive. 3., 6. Ah, but in case I stand one lit - tle chance, _

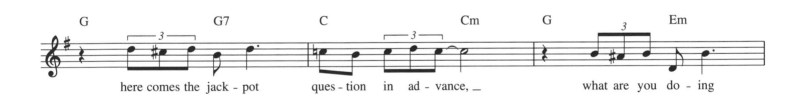

here comes the jack - pot ques - tion in ad - vance, _ what are you do - ing

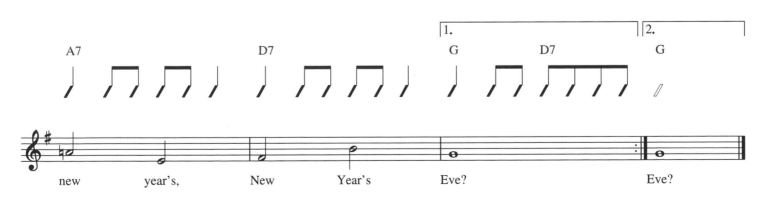

new year's, New Year's Eve? Eve?

73

When Santa Claus Gets Your Letter

Music and Lyrics by Johnny Marks

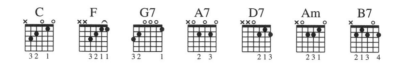

Intro
Moderately

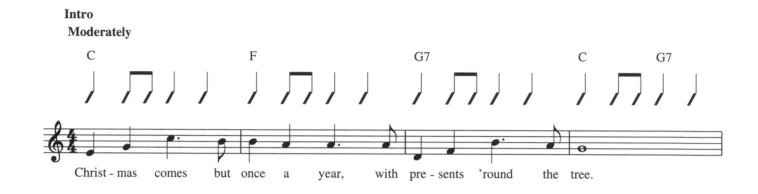

Christ-mas comes but once a year, with pre-sents 'round the tree.

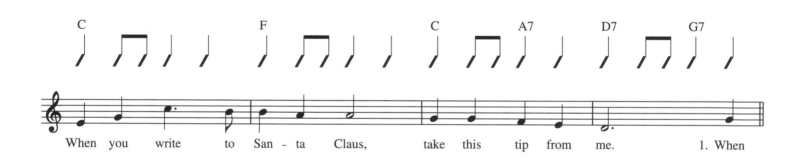

When you write to San-ta Claus, take this tip from me. 1. When

Verse

(4.) San-ta Claus gets your let-ter, you know what he will say: "Have

you been good the way you should on ev-'ry sin-gle day?" 2., 5. When

Verse

San - ta Claus gets your let - ter, to ask for Christ - mas toys, he'll

take a look in his good book he keeps for girls and boys. He'll

Bridge

stroke his beard, his eyes will glow and at your name he'll peer. It takes a lit - tle

Verse

time you know, to check back one whole year! 3., 6. When San - ta Claus gets your

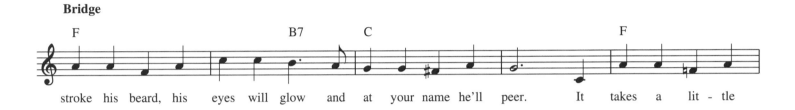

let - ter, I real - ly do be - lieve, you'll head his list, you

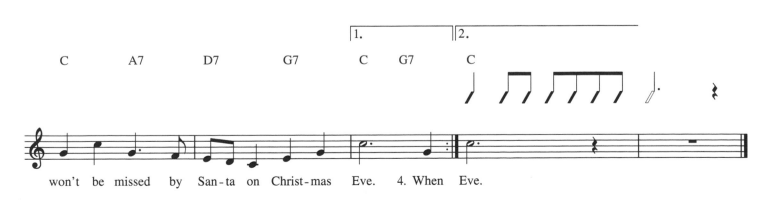

won't be missed by San - ta on Christ - mas Eve. 4. When Eve.

Wonderful Christmastime

Words and Music by McCartney

We're sim - ply hav - ing a won - der - ful Christ - mas -

D.C. al Coda
(take 2nd ending)

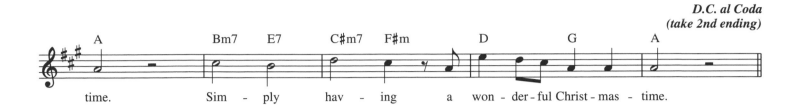

time. Sim - ply hav - ing a won - der - ful Christ - mas - time.

⊕ *Coda*

Ding dong, ding dong, ding dong, ding dong, ding dong, ding

dong, dong dong, dong, dong. The par - ty's on, ___ the spir - it's up, _

___ we're here to - night _ and that's e - nough. _

Outro-Chorus

Repeat & Fade

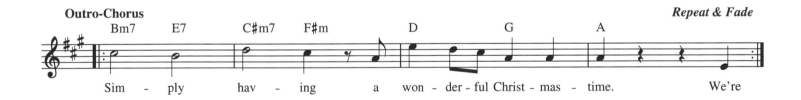

Sim - ply hav - ing a won - der - ful Christ - mas - time. We're

Additional Lyrics

2. The party's on,
   The feeling's here
   That only comes
   This time of year.

3. The word is out
   About the town,
   To lift a glass.
   Oh, don't look down.

You Make It Feel Like Christmas

Words and Music by Neil Diamond

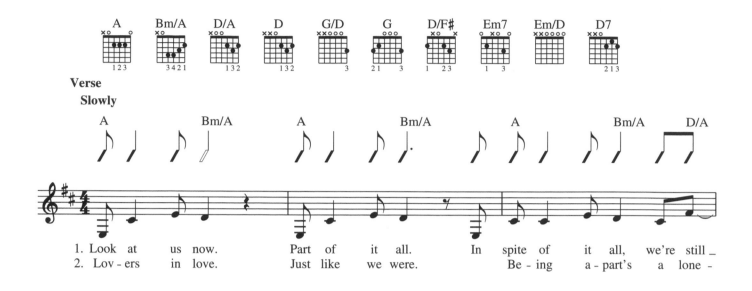

Verse
Slowly

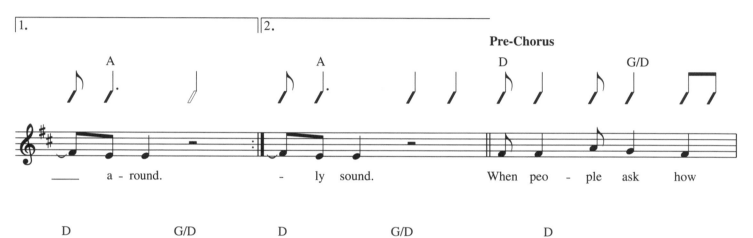

1. Look at us now. Part of it all. In spite of it all, we're still _
2. Lov - ers in love. Just like we were. Be - ing a - part's a lone -

Pre-Chorus

_ a - round. - ly sound. When peo - ple ask how

cont. rhy. sim.

we stay to - geth - er, I say you nev - er let _ me down. And

Chorus

you make it feel _ like Christ - mas e - ven when things _ go _ wrong.

_ I hear the sound _ of Christ - mas in your song _

all   year   long.

Verse

3. Look   at   the   sun   shin - ing   on   me.   No - where   could   be   a   bet -

Pre-Chorus

- ter   place.   Lov - ers   in   love.   That's what   we   are.

% **Chorus**

cont. rhy. sim.

Reach   for   that   star   out   there ___ in   space.   'Cause   you   make   it   feel ___ like   Christ -

- mas   e - ven   when   things __ go ___ wrong. ___

I   hear   the   sound _ of   Christ - mas   in   your   song ___   all   year